Lois Duncan

Other titles in the *Authors Teens Love* series:

Ray Bradbury
*Master of Science Fiction
and Fantasy*
ISBN-13: 978-0-7660-2240-9
ISBN-10:   0-7660-2240-4

Orson Scott Card
Architect of Alternate Worlds
ISBN-13: 978-0-7660-2354-3
ISBN-10:   0-7660-2354-0

Robert Cormier
Author of The Chocolate War
ISBN-13: 978-0-7660-2719-0
ISBN-10:   0-7660-2719-8

Roald Dahl
Author of Charlie and the
Chocolate Factory
ISBN-13: 978-0-7660-2353-6
ISBN-10:   0-7660-2353-2

Paula Danziger
Voice of Teen Troubles
ISBN-13: 978-0-7660-2444-1
ISBN-10:   0-7660-2444-X

S. E. Hinton
Author of The Outsiders
ISBN-13: 978-0-7660-2720-6
ISBN-10:   0-7660-2720-1

C. S. Lewis
Chronicler of Narnia
ISBN-13: 978-0-7660-2446-5
ISBN-10:   0-7660-2446-6

Lois Lowry
*The Giver of Stories and
Memories*
ISBN-13: 978-0-7660-2722-0
ISBN-10:   0-7660-2722-8

Joan Lowery Nixon
Masterful Mystery Writer
ISBN-13: 978-0-7660-2194-5
ISBN-10:   0-7660-2194-7

Gary Paulsen
*Voice of Adventure
and Survival*
ISBN-13: 978-0-7660-2721-3
ISBN-10:   0-7660-2721-X

Richard Peck
A Spellbinding Storyteller
ISBN-13: 978-0-7660-2723-7
ISBN-10:   0-7660-2723-6

Philip Pullman
Master of Fantasy
ISBN-13: 978-0-7660-2447-2
ISBN-10:   0-7660-2447-4

Jerry Spinelli
Master Teller of Teen Tales
ISBN-13: 978-0-7660-2718-3
ISBN-10:   0-7660-2718-X

R. L. Stine
*Creator of Creepy and
Spooky Stories*
ISBN-13: 978-0-7660-2445-8
ISBN-10:   0-7660-2445-8

J. R. R. Tolkien
Master of Imaginary Worlds
ISBN-13: 978-0-7660-2246-1
ISBN-10:   0-7660-2246-3

E. B. White
Spinner of Webs and Tales
ISBN-13: 978-0-7660-2350-5
ISBN-10:   0-7660-2350-8

AUTHORS TEENS LOVE

Lois Duncan

Author of *I Know What You Did Last Summer*

Kimberly Campbell

Enslow Publishers, Inc.
40 Industrial Road
Box 398
Berkeley Heights, NJ 07922
USA

http://www.enslow.com

Library of Congress Cataloging-in-Publication Data

Campbell, Kimberly, 1971–
    Lois Duncan : author of I know what you did last summer / Kimberly Campbell.
        p. cm. — (Authors teens love)
    Includes bibliographical references (p.   ) and index.
    Summary: "A biography of American author Lois Duncan"—Provided by publisher.
    ISBN-13: 978-0-7660-2963-7
    ISBN-10: 0-7660-2963-8
    1. Duncan, Lois, 1934–   —Juvenile literature. 2. Authors, American—20th century—Biography—Juvenile literature. 3. Children's stories—Authorship—Juvenile literature. I. Title.
    PS3554.U464Z625 2009
    813'.54—dc22
    [B]   2008013874

Printed in the United States of America

10 9 8 7 6 5 4 3 2 1

To Our Readers: We have done our best to make sure all Internet Addresses in this book were active and appropriate when we went to press. However, the author and publisher have no control over and assume no liability for the material available on those Internet sites or on other Web sites they may link to. Any comments or suggestions can be sent by e-mail to comments@enslow.com or to the address on the back cover.

♻ Enslow Publishers, Inc., is committed to printing our books on recycled paper. The paper in every book contains 10% to 30% post-consumer waste (PCW). The cover board on the outside of each book contains 100% PCW. Our goal is to do our part to help young people and the environment too!

Photos and Illustrations: All images courtesy of Donald Arquette and Lois Duncan, except p. 60, courtesy of the Everett Collection, Inc.

Cover Illustration: Lois Duncan (foreground photo portrait); Mark A. Hicks (background illustration).

Contents

1. An Important Visitor.............. 7
2. Little Girl Writer.................. 15
3. The Teen Years 23
4. Duke University and
   Falling in Love................... 33
5. Single and Struggling 42
6. Newlywed Again.................. 48
7. Hitting the Books 54
8. Tragedy Strikes 63
9. Trailblazer and Truth Seeker 73

In Her Own Words................ 82

Chronology 86

Selected Works by Lois Duncan... 90

Chapter Notes 93

Glossary 97

Further Reading 99

Internet Addresses................ 100

Index 101

Chapter 1

An Important Visitor

Lois Duncan Steinmetz was just ten years old when she submitted her first typed manuscript, titled "Fairy in the Woods," to *Ladies' Home Journal.* Her story was about a little boy who fell in love with a fairy. Though the story was quickly rejected, Lois received a kind letter from the editor, complimenting her on her writing, but saying the magazine was not interested in a story about the supernatural. Despite the turndown, Lois clung to her goal of becoming a published author and continued to submit manuscripts filled with violence, adventure, and romance to adult magazines. Like many grown-up writers, she would eagerly run to the mailbox every day to see if there was a letter from an editor who wanted to buy her work.

As soon as one story came back, she would

send out another in its place. Soon Lois was raking in rejection slips. Three years passed. The stack of rejection slips grew and grew. Finally, her mother made her throw them all in the trash.

At age thirteen, Lois came home from school one day to find a stranger sitting on the living-room sofa. He was MacKinlay Kantor. He was a neighbor who lived on the same beach on Siesta Key, in Sarasota, Florida. Lois was excited to learn that this visitor was a writer.

As soon as one story came back, she would send out another in its place.

"Lois, why don't you show Mr. Kantor that story that just came back from the *Saturday Evening Post*?" her father suggested.[1]

Lois ran to get the story. Her enthusiasm spilled over as she stood next to Kantor, eagerly awaiting his opinion. He slowly and carefully read her work. Finally, he looked at Lois and began, "My dear, I hate to tell you, but this is pure trash!"

"Mack!" exclaimed Lois's mother. "Lois is only thirteen!"

"I don't care how old she is," said Kantor. "If she is trying to *sell* her stories, she is old enough to be told what is wrong with them. What kind of subject matter is this for a kid? Lois has never had a love affair or seen a man be murdered. Good writing comes from the heart, not off the top of the head."

Kantor's reaction was not what Lois had expected. In fact, it stunned her. Kantor continued as kindly and truthfully as he could, saying, "Lois, good writing comes from the heart. Throw this stuff away, child, and write a story about something you know. Write something that rings *true*."[2]

Although Lois's first in-person and honest critique of her writing cut to the quick, her encounter with MacKinlay Kantor may have been the best thing that could have happened to her budding career. Although his words were harsh, they spurred her to change her subject matter. In fact, she wrote a brand-new story later that week, about an average girl involved in everyday activities and submitted it to *Calling All Girls*, a national teen publication. The title of that story was "P.S. We Are Fine." Lois described the story as "a humorous story about three children whose father gets a job transfer. The kids are left to stay with a stuffy, old-maid aunt while their parents house hunt in the town where the father now will be working. The story was written in the form of letters that the children wrote their parents, complaining, tattling on each other's misbehavior, describing finding their aunt's teeth in a glass by her bed, etc."[3]

This new and more realistic approach to writing resulted in Lois's first sale. She received a check for twenty-five dollars from *Calling All Girls*.

Recalling this, Lois said, "It was the most incredible moment of my life."[4]

Lois landed her first magazine sale due in part to Kantor's tough but honest advice: "Write from the heart about something you know."[5]

From then on, Lois's storytelling and writing skills were on a better path. With a clear head and the advice of Kantor freshly in mind, she figured out the types of stories that would probably sell and the kinds of publications most likely to buy them. It helped that she was also a tenacious girl. Now that she had been given one of the "secrets" to good writing, she let nothing hold her back. Lois rushed home from school every day and sat at her small, manual typewriter. All of the aches and pleasures of being a preteen spilled out onto the pages. She wrote about her first kiss, being heartbroken because of a boy, and the disappointment of not being invited to a friend's slumber party. She turned her own real-life heartbreaks into stories that rang true to life, sometimes with a little twist. For instance, when she did not get the lead in the school play, she wrote a story in which she did get the lead.

When Lois portrayed believable characters, settings, and everyday thoughts and feelings, a good number of her manuscripts started to sell. She sold many of her stories to major teen magazines, not because the writing was perfect, but mostly because of the realism of the subject matter.

What became of this important visitor, MacKinlay Kantor? He turned out to be one of the more prolific and successful American writers of his time. Kantor became a hugely successful writer in his own right. He won the 1956 Pulitzer Prize for his book *Andersonville,* an epic novel about the notorious Civil War prison camp in southern Georgia, where fifty thousand Northerners suffered and nearly fourteen thousand died.[6]

> She sold many of her stories . . . because of the realism of the subject matter.

Had it not been for the wise, mentoring advice of MacKinlay Kantor, Lois may not have learned at such an early age the number-one secret to writing good stories.

MacKinlay Kantor was a person Lois looked up to all her life. In a recent interview, she commented about the relationship she had with Kantor:

> Mack Kantor and his wife, Irene, were my parents' close friends, and I was good friends with their son, Tim, who was about my age. Our family often attended parties at their home, where Mack would sing and play his guitar and sometimes read aloud from a work-in-progress. So, in that way, he was a mentor and an inspiration. However, he did not continue to critique my early work.
>
> Mack Kantor was my father's best man when he remarried after the death of my mother. In 1973, when I wrote my first adult novel, WHEN THE BOUGH BREAKS, MacKinlay Kantor wrote a blurb for the jacket:
>
> "Once upon a time Lois Duncan was a darling

and darting child, and she scampered on our Florida beach; and then she began to write little-girl poems and stories, and later big-girl poems and stories, and we applauded her energy and her skill. Today she writes about grown-up issues with courage and tenderness and devotion. I am proud to be a charter member of the 'I Love Lois Duncan Club' and trust that all readers will hasten to join."[7]

Lois Duncan included this same endorsement in her book of poetry, *Seasons of the Heart* (iUniverse, 2007). Many of the poems in that book are about her own childhood days in Sarasota, Florida, where she played on the beaches. She said, "I felt certain that Mack would have wanted to have his fingerprint on that particular book."[8]

MacKinlay Kantor was a person Lois looked up to all her life.

MacKinlay Kantor died on October 11, 1977. Kantor's office, with his desk and other furniture, telephone, books, knickknacks, and pictures (some of which were taken by Lois's photographer father), has been replicated at the Sarasota County History Center. It is on display for visitors and fans.

Kantor was an inspiration to Lois. Whatever wisdom he imparted must have stuck in Lois's brain, because she went on to publish nearly fifty books and more than three hundred articles and stories, which appeared in major publications such as *Saturday Evening Post*, *Good Housekeeping*, *Redbook*, *Seventeen*, *McCalls*, *Reader's Digest*, and *Woman's Day*.[9]

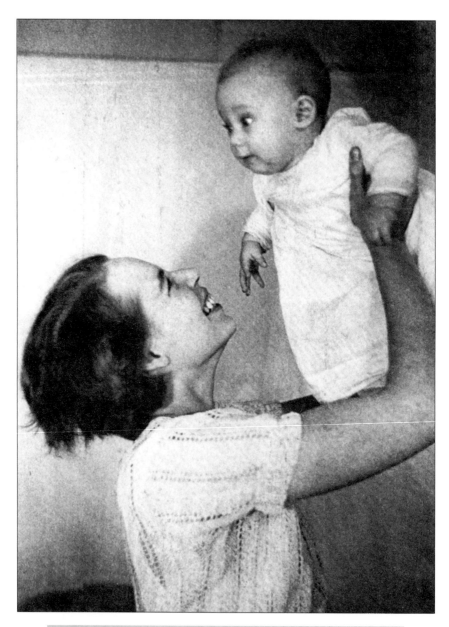

Lois Duncan Foley Steinmetz holds up her baby girl, the
future award-winning author Lois Duncan, in 1934.

Chapter 2

Little Girl Writer

Lois Duncan Steinmetz was born on April 28, 1934, in Philadelphia, Pennsylvania, to Joseph Janney Steinmetz and Lois Duncan Foley Steinmetz. Both of Lois's parents were internationally known magazine photographers. Creativity obviously ran in the family, and that gift of imagination was passed down to Lois.

Lois's mother cultivated her daughter's interest in reading. She read to Lois almost every day. As young as age two, Lois would sit beside her mother and plunge into the pleasurable world of fairytales, poetry, and picture books. At age three, she was dictating her own poems and stories to her parents. When she learned the alphabet, she wrote stories on paper all by herself.

Lois became a big sister in 1937, when her brother, Bill, was born.

During World War II, Lois's father became the chief training officer at the Naval School of Photography in Pensacola, Florida. The family became enchanted with the state of Florida and after the war they settled in a beach house on Siesta Key in Sarasota.

This part of the country was a convenient place for this particular family. It allowed Lois's parents to accept photo assignments in the southeastern parts of the United States and in the Caribbean. Lois and Bill had the luxury of going with their parents on some of these trips.

Lois Duncan as a toddler bathing in the sink in 1937.

Lois's kinfolk were all blessed with the gift of creativity which found its expression in different ways. Both Lois's grandmothers were concert pianists and her parents played musical instruments, but Lois, herself, did not have much interest in music. At bedtime, Lois much preferred a bedtime story, instead of a lullaby. Lois loved stories and tall tales.

As she grew from toddler to young girl, her delight in storytelling grew with her. Lois could be serious about it, but she also had fun with it. Some nights, in the bedroom she shared with her little brother Billy, Lois pretended she was the "Moon Fairy," coming to deliver a message that the moon was falling from the sky. "Soon it will hit the earth!" cried Lois dramatically.[1]

"And what will happen to *me*?" Billy would ask in terror.

"You'll be blown up into the sky," Lois would tell him, adding more and more scary details. The nightmarish stories got so bad that Lois and her brother were given separate bedrooms.

Even as a small child, Lois stood out from the pack. One day in kindergarten, she volunteered to recite an original poem for show-and-tell. When it was her turn to share, Lois boldly stepped to the front of the classroom and proudly recited the poem, which was about a shipwreck. When she was through, instead of praising her, the teacher crushed her spirit. The teacher claimed that five-year-old Lois could not possibly have composed that poem and must have stolen it from a

Baby brother Bill, their mother, and a young Lois stand on the beach in front of their house in Sarasota, Florida, in 1941.

published writer. Lois had worked hard on the poem, and it was her own original work. The teacher sent Lois to stand in the corner as punishment. About that day, Lois said later, "It was years before I trusted another teacher again."[2]

But lively stories were what made Lois tick. So she did not give up her love of writing and how it made her feel inside. No one could take it away, not *even* a grown-up! Not even a teacher!

Lois had a close relationship with her mother. At age ten, she wrote this poem:

"My Mother"

The noon of life is warm and deep
With all the joys that be,
And I shall have a man's love
To hold my heart for me.

The eve of life is still and cool
And drenched with memories sweet,
And I shall have my little loves,
Playing at my feet.

But, oh, it is the dawn of life
With dreams so fresh and wild,
That holds for me my first love,
Who knows me as a child,

And when the night of life is here
And stars begin to wane,

Then it will be my first love
Who takes me in again.[3]

Lois also spent time on normal childhood activities and especially enjoyed her time alone. She would ride her bike to the beach, where she would lie in the sand and daydream as she listened to the sound of the waves. When she got home, she would scribble those thoughts in notebooks. She also liked playing in the woods and had a secret hideout in the middle of a bamboo clump. She said later, "I would bend the bamboo until I could straddle it, and it would spring up, and I would slide down into the hollow at its heart with green stalks all around me and the leaves like lace against my face. I'd hide there and read."[4]

At age ten, Lois began submitting her work to magazines. It took a lot of time, dedication, and effort to write every day. She had to sacrifice some playtime in order to make progress. Lois, as an adult, remembered it this way: "When I was a kid, I came home from school each day and sat down at the typewriter, the same way kids today might turn on the television."[5]

> **At age ten, Lois began submitting her work to magazines.**

Having learned a lot from her meeting with MacKinlay Kantor, Lois rose to the challenge. She set out with passion and purpose to write from the heart. She launched a flurry of manuscript submissions. These new stories were realistic accounts of teenage life. She pulled from her own adolescent feelings, from the ups and downs of puberty.

At age twelve, she wrote this precocious and thoughtful poem.

"The Song of Life"

This is the song I am singing tonight
When the stars are pale and the sky is deep.
It's a song I have learned from all things bright,
When the weeping laugh and the laughing weep,
When the dying live and the living die,
For something is singing that's stronger than I,
Like the sun or the rain or the earth or the sky,
While the sleeping wake and the waking sleep.

This is a song of forgotten things,
The flowers of summer, the hush of the snow,
The millions of glorious, golden springs
That blossomed and faded and died long ago.
It's a song that was made when the earth was begun
Of the dances we dance and the races we run,
Of the laughter and tears that will never be done
And the millions of things that we never will know.[6]

When, at age thirteen, one of her stories sold to *Calling All Girls* magazine, Lois was overjoyed. She was finally recognized and *paid* for her work!

Lois was a teenage version of a full-fledged writer. She was an ordinary girl but had an all-consuming dream. Even at this young age, she also knew with one hundred percent certainty that she would have five children someday.

Both "gut feelings" about her future eventually would come true.

Chapter 3

The Teen Years

Now published and in her teens, Lois had to make an important decision. She needed a pen name to distinguish her from her mother, who was also named Lois Steinmetz, and who also occasionally wrote for magazines. Her mother suggested that Lois drop her last name, "Steinmetz," and write under her middle name, "Duncan," which was also her grandmother's maiden name. Lois loved the idea and, overnight, became "Lois Duncan."

Lois remembers her teenage years as idyllic. Because her parents were magazine photographers, they received assignments all over the country and, whenever possible, took Lois and Billy with them. During summer vacation, Lois and Billy could see many beautiful places and interesting people.

Lois recalls, "All my memories of my parents are happy ones. They were creative, delightful people, who worked well together as a photo team, enjoyed each other's company, and deeply loved each other and their children. Bill and I often reminisce about what a wonderful childhood we had."[1]

Lois's father was also a photographer for the Ringling Brothers Barnum and Bailey Circus. The circus spent the winter months (its off-season) in Sarasota, Florida. Her father took photographs of the circus's behind-the-scenes moments. He captured pictures of elephants climbing onto the circus train; Emmett Kelly, the clown, in a bubble bath; and the Flying Wallendas teaching their four-year-old daughter to walk the high wire.

Ringling Brothers was a part of Lois's everyday life. Some of the children of the circus performers were her classmates at Sarasota High School. One special memory stands out—something that happened after her grandmother, Perle Duncan Foley, died. Lois remembers, "My grandmother was a tiny woman with size 3 feet, and she loved to show them off. After her death, my mother was faced with the challenge of what to do with a closet filled with 40 pairs of custom-made, size-3 shoes. She ended up giving them to the midgets at Ringling Brothers. The Doll Family was thrilled! For the first time in their lives, those little women had classy shoes. Up until then they'd had to buy all their shoes in the children's department."[2]

Later in her career, Lois wrote *The Circus*

Comes Home (Doubleday, 1993), a picture book for both kids and grown-ups. It shows what the circus does behind the scenes when it is not touring the country. The book contains black-and-white photographs taken by her father in the 1940s. Steinmetz said these pictures were his favorites because they showed "The Golden Age of Circus." The pictures portray both the whimsy and the hardworking parts of circus life. The circus and her father's photographs made a strong impression on Lois.

Lois explained how this picture-book project came about. "When my father died, I fell heir to a huge box of his black and white negatives, many of them of the circus. I printed them in my home

> **The circus and her father's photographs made a strong impression on Lois.**

darkroom (a converted bathroom), and wrote text to go with them. So, after his death, my father and I collaborated on a children's picture book, *The Circus Comes Home: When the Greatest Show on Earth Rode the Rails*, by Lois Duncan with photos by Joseph Steinmetz."[3]

As a teen, Lois dove headlong into writing. Her mother would have liked her to have developed a few more hobbies, such as tennis, golf, piano, and ballet, instead of concentrating solely on writing.

But since Lois was five years old, writing had been her only dream. Her mother eventually realized that nothing could redirect her daughter's drive and passion, so she finally gave up trying to sway her. Lois recently said, "I think in her heart my mother had always wanted to be a writer but was distracted from that goal when she married my father

> **As a teen, Lois dove headlong into writing.**

and helped him establish their photography business. So she took a vicarious pleasure in my career."[4]

Despite young Lois's early success, the rejection letters still trickled in. One editor gave Lois a smart tip: "Reach into your own life." Determined to find the recipe for success, Lois did just that. She decided to write about one of the funniest experiences she had in high school. Called *Home Economics Report*, it was written about the trials and tribulations in her home economics class. Lois described the skirt she could not finish hemming, no matter how many hours she stitched. She worked on hemming that skirt all semester! The problem was, she had forgotten to knot the thread!

This story earned Lois fifty dollars from *Senior Prom* magazine. Even though she flunked the class (and was the only girl in the class who did), she was able to turn the experience into a humorous story. It is a tale that she shares with her fans to this day. After the story was published, Lois

Lois, at age fourteen, daydreams in a tree. By 1948, she was selling her stories to national magazines such as *Calling All Girls*.

received mail from other high school girls across the country who hated "home ec."

At age sixteen, Lois won second place in *Seventeen* magazine's annual short-story contest. At age seventeen, she won third place, and finally, at age eighteen, she won the top slot—first place! The title of her first-place entry was "Return." It was a story about a Korean War veteran adjusting to civilian life. Throughout her high school years, Lois wrote regularly for teen publications, most notably *Seventeen* magazine.

Lois wrote regularly for teen publications, most notably *Seventeen* magazine.

In high school, Lois's braces came off just about the time her adolescent baby fat disappeared. Lois happily discovered that she was pretty. In many and most ways, she was a typical teenager. Lois giggled at and admired the cute boys she met. She kept busy with her girlfriends too.

Lois dated many boys. There are references to several of them in poems in *Seasons of the Heart*. Lois explains:

> This was an era in which boys and girls mingled and mixed. We had dance cards at proms so we didn't have to dance all night with one person. One of my most interesting high school boyfriends was Arnold Mandell, who was the most brilliant person I've ever

known, even at age 14. He grew up to become Professor of Psychiatry, Neurosciences, Physiology and Pharmacology at the University of California Medical School in San Diego. In my senior year, my boyfriend was Sumner Darling, who grew up to become a well-known architect. I had no interest in dating "jocks"; I wanted boyfriends with brains who were interesting to talk to.[5]

At the age of seventeen, she wrote this dreamy poem about falling in love.

"Love in March"

Falling in love is a kite in the wind,
Tugging and straining to get to the sun,
Daring and dipping and doubling back—
"Is this forever? Can he be the one?"
Plunging toward earth as the breezes go slack—
"Gosh, he's so quiet. He thinks I'm a bore.
No—now he's smiling! He likes me again!"
Caught from beneath and sent soaring once more.
Falling in love is a hazardous thing—
All of your dreams on the end of a string.[6]

Lois's best friend in high school was Christia Basler, whose family owned a small dairy farm on the edge of town. This is where Lois learned to milk a cow. Ironically, Christia was not allowed to milk the cows because she was a musician who played piano and organ. Her parents were afraid she would hurt her hands milking cows!

Although Lois enjoyed the fun times, there were serious things happening in the world around her. When she was in high school, the Korean War began. Lois and her friends dated some of the soldiers who were training near her Sarasota, Florida, home. Lois worried about what these young men would have to face when they were shipped overseas to fight in combat.[7]

Lois remembers, "The war was a fact of life for us—always on our minds, like a black cloud hanging over us—but, thankfully, no one I loved was injured or killed."[8]

> ## "The war was a fact of life for us."
> ### —Lois Duncan

In her senior year of high school, Lois had her sights set on being editor of the school newspaper, but she did not get the job. In those days, a boy always filled the post. During the 1950s, girls were not treated fairly. Even so, Lois was still surprised that she did not get the job, because she felt she was the most qualified. She was the only person in her high school whose work had been published. Luckily, she was assigned to another position on the school's newspaper. Lois called it "the next best job."[9] She was made "managing editor." She soon realized it was the better job since it required hands-on work. She learned to design layouts, write headlines, and condense long stories to fit the available space. Lois admits now, "That was better than being a figurehead!"[10]

Lois kept plugging away with her writing. In fact, she cranked out so much good material by

Lois and her date, Sumner Darling, attend their high school prom in 1952.

this point that she made enough money *selling* her work to be able to buy her own Jeep! This was quite an accomplishment at the time. Not many teenagers had cars—especially girls. Lois would drive her Jeep to beach parties and take her friends to drive-in movies too. Her popularity at school soared because of that Jeep.

Lois graduated from Sarasota High School in 1952 and headed to college at Duke University in North Carolina.

Chapter 4

Duke University and Falling in Love

Education was a strong tradition in the Steinmetz family. Duncan's parents were well-educated, and they expected the same for their children. Her father had graduated from Princeton, one of the Ivy League schools. Her mother graduated from Smith College in Massachusetts. Duncan's parents decided that she should attend Duke University in North Carolina. It was close enough so she could easily come home for vacations, and the university had a good reputation.

For many years, the Steinmetz family had saved money and built up a college fund for Duncan. Even though Duncan was offered a scholarship, her parents would not let her accept it. They believed it was morally wrong to accept a scholarship that could go to somebody needier—a person who honestly could not afford to pay the tuition.

Upon arriving on the Duke campus in 1952, Duncan discovered something surprising—she did not feel comfortable there. She discovered that dormitory living permitted no privacy and prevented the downtime that she needed to be creative. She could not concentrate with so much commotion and noise going on around her. She described it as too much togetherness.

Duncan could not stay alone in her room for more than twenty minutes without being disturbed. She said, "Two dozen well-meaning dorm mates would ask anxiously what the matter was."[1] The girls would knock on Duncan's door to find out if she was "all right in there." It distracted Duncan and kept her from being able to focus.

She was also annoyed with herself because she could not easily remember people's names. And with so many girls swarming here and there and everywhere, she was quite frustrated in her new environment.

Her creativity depended on time by herself, which was impossible in the college atmosphere. Being alone was simply impossible at Duke University. From classes, to sororities, to parties— everything was focused on being part of a group.

Duncan was desperate to get back to writing stories. She waited until Christmas to tell her parents that she wanted to drop out of college. When she did, her parents were greatly dismayed. "But if you drop out, what will you do?" they asked fretfully.[2]

Duncan's parents had every right to be concerned. These were the days when women rarely supported themselves and had very few career choices. Also, in the 1950s, people thought that an unmarried woman who lived on her own was a misfit. Most women lived at home until they got married because society demanded it. The expectation was for women to marry a good man and become homemakers. Men were usually the sole moneymakers.

Duncan was desperate to get back to writing stories.

This left Duncan with a tough decision. For a variety of reasons, it made sense to remain in college. She did not want to move back home and live under her parents' roof. She wanted to grow up and be a part of the adult world she had daydreamed about for so many years.

Duncan decided to honor her parents' wishes and reluctantly went back to Duke. She made the honor roll for her first semester.

At the start of the college year, Duncan had begun dating a good-looking senior named Joseph "Buzz" Cardozo. Duncan described him as "attractive, intelligent, and charming."[3] And "persuasive."

That spring, Buzz proposed and Duncan accepted. Saying yes to marriage seemed like a good idea at the time.

> **Saying yes to marriage seemed like a good idea at the time.**

At the end of her freshman year, Duncan dropped out of school to marry Cardozo. Duncan's parents were not happy about this turn of events, but they made the best of it, and gave their daughter a nice wedding. Cardozo and Duncan were married on May 2, 1953, in the Duke University Chapel. At age nineteen, Lois Duncan was officially no longer a college student.

Instead of an exotic honeymoon trip, the young couple focused on life's more urgent and practical matters. Cardozo still had to graduate. So, they rented an apartment near the campus and he finished out the school year.

While her husband finished classes at Duke to earn his college degree, Duncan quickly became a dutiful wife. Cardozo enlisted in the U. S. Air Force. The first two years of their marriage, Duncan was an air force wife. The couple moved from town to town as Cardozo was transferred from one military base to another.

Duncan was in charge of housekeeping, which bored her to death. She also developed a major case of writer's block. She wanted to snap out of her funk, but did not know how.

Her frustration was reflected in one of the few poems she wrote during that time period:

The Faithful Wife

Oh, it's many a mile and it's many a mile
To the wondrous land of Spain,
But I have stood on a Spanish hill
And laughed in the silver rain;
I have crouched in a Spanish fort
And heard the cannons roar
And spent the night 'neath crimson sheets
In the arms of a matador.

Oh, it's many a mile and it's many a mile
To the splendid China wall,
But I have eaten toasted snails
And slept in a silken shawl;
I have listened to peacocks scream
And watched the coolies flee
And found my live with a Chinese prince
In the shade of a mulberry tree.

Oh, it's many a mile from our kitchen door
To half the world away.
I lie at night in the curve of your arm,
And I cook your meals by day.
All of my life I give to you
And glad that it may be so,
But my heart goes roaming many a mile
That you will never know.[4]

In 1954, her daughter Robin was born and Duncan was suddenly rejuvenated. At age twenty, she was filled with a new zest for writing, possibly because of the joy she took in motherhood. Although she had less time now to write, she made the most of it. She decided to start a novel. Being close to the teen years herself, it made sense for Duncan to write a story from a teenage point of view. After all, she had had more experience being a teen than an adult.

When Cardozo was discharged from the service, he entered Stetson law school in St. Petersburg, Florida. Unfortunately, he started acting like a college student again. He was gone a lot. He was either in class, studying, or hanging out with his single friends. In his spare time, he played tennis, water-skied, and went to parties. Meanwhile, Duncan stayed home with their baby.

To fill the empty and lonesome hours, Duncan continued work on her novel, a teenage love story. In 1956, after the birth of her second daughter, Kerry, the novel was completed. She titled it *Debutante Hill*, and entered it in the "Seventeenth Summer Literary Contest," sponsored by publisher Dodd, Mead. She dedicated the novel to her mother. The story is about pretty, popular Lynn Chambers, who is a senior in high school when the mother of an unpopular girl decides to introduce debutantes in Rivertown. The boy Lynn had dated junior year is away at college, and the excitement of making a debut seems a wonderful way of filling a lonely time. Then Lynn's doctor father

Lois Duncan sits in the backyard of her Florida home, behind her typewriter, with her two daughters, Robin (left) and Kerry. In 1956, she completed her first novel *Debutante Hill*, which was published two years later.

denounces debutantes as "undemocratic" and forbids her to become one. Cut off from her regular social circle, Lynn has to make new friends and learn about the lifestyles of people who are not from her privileged background.

Between changing diapers and being a loving mother, Duncan waited patiently at home for the results of the writing contest. She also did what all authors do every day: she checked the mailbox for news on her submissions. Finally, word came from the contest judges. They liked Duncan's story but were reluctant to publish it because it contained a scene in which a nineteen-year-old boy drank a beer. Back then, editors did not approve of mentioning liquor in a youth novel.

> **Duncan was filled with joy on the day that she held her first bound novel.**

Duncan changed the word "beer" to "Coke" and her entry won the contest.

Duncan pocketed a thousand dollars and was offered her first young adult novel contract. *Debutante Hill* was published in 1958. Duncan was filled with joy on the day that she held her first bound novel. Being a published author in your early twenties was (and still is) a remarkable feat.

With Cardozo so busy and away from the house so often, Duncan focused on her children and her writing projects. Meanwhile, Cardozo finished law school and became an attorney. After that, Duncan says, "He was so busy, I hardly saw him."[5]

On the surface, all seemed fine and normal. But Duncan knew that her relationship with Cardozo was beginning to crumble. For years, Cardozo and Duncan lived virtually separate lives. He was busy being an attorney and a party person, and she was busy writing books and being involved with the day-to-day needs of their children.

In 1960, their first son, Brett Duncan, was born. For the sake of the children, Duncan tried to pretend that everything was all right in her marriage. She was unhappy, but even so, Duncan continued to write both novels and picture books.

When Duncan was twenty-seven, she discovered that her husband had fallen in love with another woman. Duncan was devastated. There was nothing she could do to fix it. Her marriage was over.

Chapter 5

Single and Struggling

Duncan was embarrassed to be divorced. She had never known a divorced person. Divorce was a fairly unusual event back in the early 1960s. As Duncan herself said, "Marriages were expected to last forever."[1]

Heartsick and worried about her future, Duncan had to decide what to do next. With her marriage ending and her future uncertain, she had to come up with a way to support herself and her children. With no training, no college degree, and no work experience, she was facing long, tough odds.

So, in 1962, Duncan left Florida in search of a new life and a fresh start. She uprooted herself and her three young children and headed to Albuquerque, New Mexico. Her younger brother

Bill lived there, and she wanted to be near him. It seemed like the perfect place to begin again. Being reunited with her brother was certainly helpful, but there were many serious hurdles to jump before she could relax.

Duncan now knew what it meant to fall on hard times. Her main concern was trying to eke out a living for herself and her children. Her ex-husband initially sent a few support checks, but those soon stopped.

Despite a promising writing career, Duncan had to quickly find a *real* job, with regular income. With only a handful of books to her name, the income and royalties from these books were not nearly enough to support a family of four. Her tiny royalty checks were only bringing in about two thousand dollars per year—not enough to live on.

A college education would have come in handy, as would work experience. Duncan had neither. Trying to find a job was an uphill battle, with her only real skills being writing and homemaking. After a nerve-racking search, at last she was offered a job at a small advertising company. She answered phones, ran errands, and was given some editing responsibilities. She wrote stories at night and on weekends to make extra cash to supplement her small salary.

Duncan soon wrote *Season of the Two-Heart* (Dodd, Mead, 1965). The protagonist in this book is a Pueblo teenager who leaves her reservation. She decides to live with a "white" family in order to attend public high school in Albuquerque, New

Mexico. Just as Duncan did, the girl ends up having to choose between a marriage proposal and her dream of graduating from college.

Duncan found writing difficult during this time. Late at night—after dinner, bath time, story time, and tucking in the kids—Duncan tried to burn the midnight oil at her writing desk. "I sat like a zombie in front of the typewriter and often ended up asleep with my head on the keyboard."[2]

Duncan always looked for new ways to earn extra money, so she began entering contests. With little time during the day, and being exhausted at night, she had to be creative to squeeze this activity into her hectic schedule. Being tenacious and determined, she figured out a plan that worked. She used her lunch hour at work as time she could devote to entering contests.

> **Duncan found writing difficult during this time.**

Duncan entered and won the *True Story* contest for her "most frightening experience" (a one-hundred word or less story), which earned her five hundred dollars. But there was a problem. She could not find the prize money. The envelope containing the check had accidentally been thrown out! Her oldest daughter, Robin, had dutifully taken out the garbage and deposited it in one of the cans behind their apartment complex. While Duncan held the flashlight they all took turns digging through garbage cans late at night. While halfway through the fifteenth can, they finally found the envelope with the five-hundred-dollar check inside. It had been underneath somebody's leftover spaghetti. Duncan was elated. Five hundred dollars was about two months' salary!

Duncan then won a photography contest for "Happy snapshots taken on vacation in Florida." First prize was a live, trained porpoise from Marineland! This prize was not too appealing to Duncan, who had no idea what to do with such a creature, especially since she lived in the mountains and deserts of the Southwest. Luckily, the contest coordinators gave her the option of receiving a cash prize of one thousand dollars instead of keeping the porpoise.

With a nest egg from these two contests, Duncan felt confident. She decided it was definitely time to quit her day job. The next day, she bought every magazine on the newsstands and quickly learned how to put together a good confession story. Duncan described confessions as "sensational dramas of sin and suffering, written in first person as though they were true."[3] But the stories were fiction. Duncan has said, "I wasn't putting anything over on anybody. Those stories were submitted as fiction, despite the fact that the magazine represented them as fact."

From that day on, she woke up every morning, brushed her teeth, sat down at her writing desk and wrote confessions. These stories had outrageous titles such as "I Carry a Dreadful Disease" and "Two Men Claim Me as Their Wife." None of the stories had her name on them as the author. Duncan was grateful for the anonymity. Almost all of the stories sold, and the resulting income gave Duncan the ability to buy a house and move out of her dreary apartment.

Being tenacious and determined, she figured out a plan that worked.

Duncan recently remembered those trying days when money was tight. She said:

> Those stories sold for about $200, and I wrote one per week. $800 a month meant a lot more then than it does today, but it was not a lot for a family of four. We lived frugally. Even today, my daughter, Kerry, refuses to eat noodles, because, she says, "We ate so many of them in our poor days that I'm sick of them." On the other hand, all three of those children remember with delight the wondrous thing that occurred whenever I made a "big sale" or got an advance on a book. They would come home from school, go into their rooms to change out of their school clothes, and—there are on their beds—would be a pile of new clothes and new toys. It was as if Santa Claus had come. And they never knew when it would happen! (And neither did I.)[4]

For two years Duncan cranked out stories and had very little social life. Her daily schedule consisted of being a single mother who was glued to the typewriter whipping out stories filled with imaginary misdeeds.

One day, her brother, Bill, felt sorry for her. He suggested that they go to a party at the local military base so he could introduce his sister to some nice bachelors. He introduced Duncan to a man who would soon play a very important role in her life.

Chapter 6

Newlywed Again

$\mathcal{D}$uncan described meeting Don Arquette this way:

> My brother, who was working for Sandia Laboratories on Kirtland Air Force Base, thought I needed more of a social life and took me to Happy Hour at the club on base where Sandia employees congregated on Friday evenings. He introduced me to a group of bachelor engineers, one of whom was Don Arquette, who worked in missile design. I belonged to a bridge group, composed of single people, and we were always looking for subs. When I found out that Don played bridge, I invited him to fill in the gap the next time one of the regulars could not make it. He was a better player than anyone there and soon became a regular himself.[1]

Duncan and Arquette immediately hit it off. Duncan does not ever remember a formal first date with him. Her relationship with Arquette blossomed more naturally. They were friends first. Arquette would pick her up and they would drive to the bridge game together. Duncan said, "Sometimes we would have dinner at my house first or go out for a drink afterward."[2]

Their friendship bloomed into a two-year courtship, slowly turning romantic. Duncan admired many of Arquette's personal qualities. He was stable, honest, intelligent, and dedicated to family. They also shared the same sense of humor.

Duncan and Arquette both continued to date other people. Then one night Arquette proposed.

They eventually married in 1965. Soon after, Arquette adopted Duncan's three children from her first marriage, Robin, Kerry, and Brett. Duncan relinquished the role of family provider. Her husband suggested that she stop writing confession stories and try writing for mainstream magazines, like *Good Housekeeping* and *Ladies' Home Journal*. At first, Duncan hesitated, afraid that she could not sell to those magazines because she had not been able to do so when she was younger. However, she agreed to give it a try.

Duncan wrote a two-page personal experience piece called, "The Year I Won the Contest," and mailed it to *Good Housekeeping*. (The story was about the porpoise she had won a few years before by entering a photography contest.) Duncan was flabbergasted when a check arrived for three times the amount she was used to being paid for her confession stories.

It dawned on Duncan that during all the years

of writing confessions, she had mastered her craft. She had taught herself how to plot, develop characters, create believable dialogue, and pace a story to build to a dramatic climax. These skills could be used in other writing genres (not just fiction). After that, she never wrote another confession story. She aimed future article submissions at well-paying national women's magazines that had good reputations.

> **It dawned on Duncan . . . she had mastered her craft.**

Duncan also returned to writing novels for teens, a hobby she dearly loved. But this time she wrote with an "edgier flair" and in her own style. The timing was good, since the topics that were then being written about in teenage novels were not as straight-laced and conservative as before. Writers could now write mostly about whatever they wanted, even if the story line included the word "beer." In her library research, Duncan was relieved. She found books about drug abuse, alcoholism, racial conflicts, sex, divorce, and other serious subjects that used to be taboo. Apparently, the publishing industry was now less inclined to print sugarcoated, Pollyanna-style stories for teenage audiences.

This discovery left Duncan free to write on any topic she chose, which led to the publication of *Ransom* (Doubleday, 1966). *Ransom* is an adventure

A photograph of the entire Duncan-Arquette family in 1973. Kerry and Brett are standing in the back. Don, Jr., sits on his father's lap and Kaitlyn sits with Duncan. Duncan's oldest daughter, Robin, sits to the right of her mother and baby sister.

story about teenagers kidnapped by their school bus driver. The book was very successful and was runner-up for the Edgar Allan Poe Award (presented by the Mystery Writers of America). Duncan's popularity grew as librarians across the nation stocked her new book.

When Duncan wrote *They Never Came Home* (Doubleday, 1968), literary experts took notice of this novel. This book was also a runner-up for the Edgar Allen Poe Award.

> ## When Duncan wrote *They Never Came Home*, literary experts took notice.

Duncan and Arquette had two children together: Don, Jr., in 1967 and Kaitlyn in 1970. They were a happy family. Duncan's childhood predictions had come true: she had become a writer *and* the mother of five children.

Then, came a time of sorrow. Duncan's mother died. With the loss of her mother and dearest friend, Duncan experienced numbing emotional pain. At first, she was so overcome by grief that she could barely function. Her sorrow resulted in another bad case of writer's block.

Eventually, Duncan returned to everyday life— she had to. She was a busy mother and wife. But she was still unable to be creative. At last, she decided the solution might be to change genres.

Lois Duncan on the Dreamworks set in 2008, where she got to meet the canine stars of the movie based upon her 1971 novel, *Hotel for Dogs*.

Her new book would be funny and lighthearted. Duncan was actually surprised when it was published. *Hotel for Dogs* (Houghton Mifflin, 1971) did not receive much recognition at the time it was written. Duncan never could have guessed that, thirty-five years later, the story about two children who convert an empty house into a shelter for unwanted dogs would become a major motion picture (Dreamworks, 2009).

Chapter 7

Hitting the Books

One day, Duncan received a call from a writer friend, Tony Hillerman, chairman of the journalism department at the University of New Mexico. Hillerman wanted to know if Duncan would consider teaching a class in magazine writing. Duncan was intimidated by the prospect. She felt she was not well-enough educated to be a teacher. Plus, she was a shy person. Duncan asked her husband for advice. Arquette said, "Give it a try. What's there to lose?"[1]

So, in 1971, Duncan stepped out of her comfort zone and became a lecturer for the university's journalism department. She held this part-time position for eleven years. During those years, Professor Hillerman became a best-selling author of mystery novels. Duncan was amazed at her

Duncan sailing at an outing following a writers' conference
in New England, 1973.

friend's ability to switch genres. She recalls, "I asked Tony, why, with his extensive background in journalism, he had suddenly decided to write fiction. He told me, 'A journalist is restricted to reporting facts. A fiction writer can *create* facts. That's a lot more fun.'"[2] The college bug bit Duncan. She had always felt a bit guilty about having dropped out of college and now decided to pick up where she left off. She enrolled at the University of New Mexico and took on a dual role of both lecturer and student.

Although she enjoyed learning, Duncan says that being a middle-aged woman in college was a strange experience. Not only was she older than most of her student-peers, but at times she was taking a class with some of her own students. When she signed up for a class in juvenile literature, under her married name, "Lois Arquette," she discovered that the class was studying books by "Lois Duncan." Without revealing the fact that she was the author of those books, she wrote insightful and complimentary reviews. Needless to say, she got an A.

While attending college, Duncan took a course in news photography so that she could illustrate her magazine articles. She did well in the class, and it was a help that she had had photo-journalists for parents and had learned from them the knack of composing a good picture. Midway through the class, she was hooked on this new pastime and began submitting photos to magazines. Her husband,

Duncan celebrates her graduation from the University of New Mexico in 1977.

ever supportive, converted their extra bathroom into a darkroom.

Her book for young children, *From Spring to Spring* (Westminster Press, 1982), is composed of Duncan's poems and illustrated by full-page black and white photographs. Duncan has said, "I was proud of that little book, because it was so different from anything I'd ever done."[3]

In 1977, at the age of forty-three, Duncan finally graduated cum laude with a bachelor's degree in English.

Duncan stayed true to her first love—writing. Immediately upon graduation, she sat down at her desk and wrote, "A Graduate in the Family," and sold the article to *Good Housekeeping* magazine. The payment covered the cost of her entire tuition.

Meanwhile, at home, Duncan was a typical homemaker. She did laundry, kissed boo-boos, cooked big meals, and was in the carpool line at her kids' schools. The Arquettes were a normal American family, who took vacations together, visited relatives, and enjoyed campouts and ski trips.

By the early 1980s, her hard work and perseverance were paying off. She admits that her past grind of writing fast and furiously and pumping out article after article had helped her become a better writer. And having dabbled in writing several different types of books, she ultimately found a niche in the mystery genre. She started winning awards for her scary and suspenseful "thriller" novels, many of which included a touch of the supernatural.[4]

Some of her most memorable books were filmed for television. First there was *Summer of Fear* (Little, Brown, 1976) retitled as *Stranger in Our House*. Next, was *Killing Mr. Griffin* (Little, Brown, 1978), a story about five teenagers who set out to scare their strict and hard-nosed English teacher, but end up accidentally killing him.

Realizing what it took to hold the attention of teenagers, and competing with the lure of television, Duncan was savvy enough to make her first lines pop. Here is the attention-grabbing opening line of *Killing Mr. Griffin*:

> It was a wild, windy, southwester spring when the idea of killing Mr. Griffin occurred to them.[5]

Duncan wrote *Gallows Hill* (Delacorte, 1997), which was retitled and aired as the NBC television movie, *I've Been Waiting For You* (1998).

Duncan was savvy enough to make her first lines pop.

Don't Look Behind You (Delacorte, 1989) was also made into a movie for the Fox Family Channel in 1999.

Throughout her career, Duncan has been able to publish about a book a year. She has produced entertaining stories with gripping plots that have

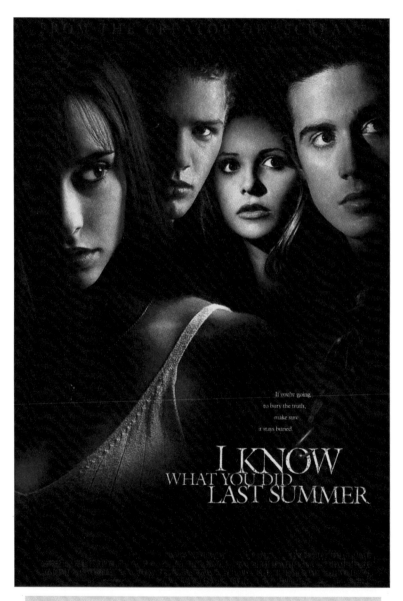

The movie poster for the 1997 film adaptation of Lois Duncan's *I Know What You Did Last Summer*.

thrilled teenagers and propelled her to worldwide fame. Interestingly, many of her books became more successful many years after they were initially published because of the hit movie based on her book *I Know What You Did Last Summer* (Little, Brown, 1973). Mandalay Productions filmed the big-screen version in 1997, more than twenty years after Duncan's novel was first published.

In one form or another, creativity definitely runs in the family. Duncan's children are gifted in music, as were most of her ancestors. From their early years they sang and played instruments and filled their house with music. Duncan took great joy in hearing them.

In a special project to honor her first grandchild (born to Kerry), Duncan and her oldest daughter, Robin Arquette, collaborated on a recording of lullabies for the new baby. They titled the recording *Songs from Dreamland* (Knopf, 1988). Duncan wrote the lyrics and was the narrator. Robin composed the music, sang all the vocals, and performed all the instrumentals.

Songs from Dreamland was first published as a book and cassette package, received excellent reviews and sold well until the second printing, when the book was accidentally packaged with the wrong cassette! The tape of sweet lullaby music was replaced with a cassette about a pig and his barnyard pals. Harsh "oinking" and farm animal noises screeched from this new tape. It certainly did not lull babies to sleep. Sales dropped off fast. This disaster caused the publisher to snatch the product out of stores. What should have been a winning partnership and product resulted in disappointment for this mother-daughter team—all due to a manufacturing mistake that could not be undone. Robin Arquette went on to create more recordings. Her enchanting songs, including the original *Songs from Dreamland* tape, can be heard on her Web site.

Having raised all five of their children by the late 1980s, Duncan and Arquette were ready to enjoy retirement and their new empty nest.

Little did they know that an unimaginable nightmare was on the horizon. In an even crueler twist of fate, Duncan would soon learn that there was a spine-chilling connection between certain details in her latest book, *Don't Look Behind You* (Delacorte, 1989) and the true-life horror story that lay ahead.

It was almost more than a mother and father could bear.

Chapter 8

Tragedy Strikes

As the summer of 1989 approached, Duncan's career was in full swing. She was writing books, articles, and poetry, and her photographs were selling to national magazines. Family life was busy too. Her youngest daughter, Kaitlyn, had just graduated with honors from high school and had enrolled in college at the University of New Mexico. Duncan and her husband assumed that, with their youngest child almost raised and headed out the door for college, a new, less stressful chapter of their lives was beginning.

In June 1989, *Don't Look Behind You* (Delacorte, 1989), Duncan's latest thriller-suspense novel, hit the bookstores. The main character, April Corrigan, was modeled upon Kaitlyn. In the story, April leads a charmed life. She is a star tennis player for her high school. She dates a neat guy. She lives in an upper-middle-class neighborhood in Virginia. Everything is nearly perfect in April's world. Her friends even call her "Princess" as a joke. One day, life as she knows it bottoms out. She is shocked to learn that her father is an undercover agent working for the FBI. Because of his knowledge of an international drug operation, the family is forced to enter the Federal Witness Protection program. They are relocated to a dreary town in central Florida, leaving behind their home, friends, and even their real names. Life goes from bad to worse. April is told that playing competitive tennis is out of the question, and contacting her old friends is impossible if she wants to keep herself and her family safe. Missing the senior prom and tennis tournaments is one thing, but being chased and hunted by a hit man named Mike Vamp, who is trying to kill April and her entire family to keep them quiet, is beyond belief.

April Corrigan was modeled upon Kaitlyn.

April, driven by anger and the desire to restore her old life, takes matters into her own hands. Against clear instructions from her parents and the FBI, she returns to Virginia in hopes of living with her grandmother and reuniting with her old boyfriend. She quickly learns that life has moved on without her and realizes that it was a bad mistake to have returned to her old hometown. She knows she must go back to Florida, but having revealed herself at her grandmother's home, she has allowed Mike Vamp to zero in on her. He is now trying to kill her and find her family. In order to save herself and her family, she outsmarts the hit man and kills him in self defense.

Duncan soon discovered that her book of fiction would have an unintended and eerie connection to her own real life.

On July 16, 1989, a month after *Don't Look Behind You* was published, Duncan's eighteen-year-old daughter, Kait, was chased down in her small car on the streets of Albuquerque, New Mexico, and shot twice in the head. The only witness was allowed to leave the scene without questioning.

Kait was rushed to University of New Mexico Hospital where she was in a coma and clung to life with the help of a respirator. After twenty hours, she was pronounced dead. Duncan and her family were by Kait's side to say goodbye. Duncan told her daughter, "Go with God."[1]

In the span of one day, Duncan's world was shattered forever. It was like a nightmare come to life.

No words comforted Duncan and her family. The agony they felt was almost too painful to bear. Near the end of the memorial service, the lullabies from *Songs from Dreamland* were played. The minister said, "And now, for the final time, Kait's beloved sister, Robin, will sing her to sleep."[2]

The police called Kait's murder a "random

Kait's car window after her violent murder.

drive-by shooting." Duncan and her family refused to accept that scenario because of strong evidence that the shooting was anything *but* random.

Through their own investigative efforts, the Arquettes learned that Kait's boyfriend of almost two years, Dung Ngoc Nguyen, a Vietnamese immigrant, had been involved in insurance fraud and drug trafficking. Duncan and Arquette believed that Kait was planning to tell authorities about this Vietnamese crime ring. They said the police ignored theories that pointed to the Vietnamese mafia.

Suspicion grew as Duncan's family learned more about Nguyen's background, his acquaintances, the inconsistent statements he made about his relationship with Kait, and about the night of the murder.

The family also learned that Kait and Nguyen had fought and argued. Things had gotten so bad between them, that Kait would run to the apartment manager at night, begging to sleep on his sofa because she was afraid. The family learned that Kait had accompanied Nguyen to California, where he had participated in a car-wreck insurance scam. He and his friends had staged auto accidents to make money by defrauding insurance companies.

The family could not make sense of what had happened to Kait. She did not do drugs or drink. She was a good girl, who was headed to college. She wanted to be a doctor. How could she have become entangled with such people?

Duncan worked tirelessly to find out more about Kait's daily activities, because she hoped it would lead to answers about why she was killed. Duncan spoke with Kait's friends, examined her daughter's phone records, and covered the town with reward fliers asking the public for leads. No matter what new clues Duncan and her family came up with, the police were unwilling to listen or follow up. No one, especially the police, could seem to answer the question, "Why would someone kill Kait?"

Frustrated and wanting so badly to know the truth, Duncan turned to psychic detectives and private investigators for help. Some of the psychics

Lois Duncan and Kait at age thirteen.

were able to provide useful clues, predictions, and information about the case.[3]

In a recent interview, Duncan said, "Our current belief is that Kait was killed by a hit man like Mike Vamp in my novel *Don't Look Behind You*, because she had learned too much about a variety of illegal activities, some of which were linked to her boyfriend and his friends." Kait had announced she was breaking up with Nguyen on the night of the murder.

At one point in the investigation, three Hispanic men were arrested for Kait's murder. Incredibly, the nickname of the alleged triggerman was "Mike Vamp." These men were released and charges were dropped due to lack of evidence. Still, the police refused to believe any theory other than that the crime was a random, drive-by shooting.

For many months after the death of her daughter, Duncan was unable to write. She was too brokenhearted and grief-stricken to be able to focus. The quest for information regarding Kait's violent death consumed every ounce of her energy.

Duncan eventually had the strength to express her feelings through poetry. She wrote this poem in 1990.

"The First Snow"

It snowed last night,
So this morning I went to the cemetery
To sweep the snow from her grave marker.
Ice had formed in the letters that spelled her name.

When I sat on the ice to melt it, she was mortified.
I heard her voice shriek with the sleek, black crows—
"*Nobody* else's *mother* squats in a graveyard!"[4]

Duncan started keeping meticulous notes in an effort to keep a solid record of the investigation of Kait's murder. To deal with her heartache and to prevent the facts from being buried and forgotten, Duncan wrote a nonfiction book about the whole ordeal.

On Kait's twenty-first birthday, she brought the manuscript to the cemetery before going to the post office to mail it. She told Kait, "This is your present, honey. Mother is going to get your killer."[5] Four days later, Duncan traveled to New York to discuss the book with her publisher and present the documentation to support her allegations.[6]

Who Killed My Daughter? (Delacorte, 1992) was by far the most difficult book that Duncan had ever written. It was her effort to document all that had happened. She compiled a timeline of events and clues surrounding her daughter's death in a heart-wrenching, yet understandable way. Although the book was not directly aimed at teenagers, it was named a *School Library Journal* "Best Book of the Year" and an American Library Association "Best Adult Book for Young Adults."

Duncan said that adrenaline kept her going long enough to finish the book. But her health finally gave way soon after she finished *Who Killed My Daughter?* One night as she was cooking dinner, she had a mild stroke. After a brief stay in

WHO
KILLED
MY
DAUGHTER?

"This book will break your heart....No book equals this one for credibility, bleak truth and mind-chilling horror. You will both weep and cheer for the feisty mother who seeks answers at any cost. I have read 2,000 homicide case files. Not one gripped me as this book did."
—Ann Rule,
best-selling author
of *Small Sacrifices*

BY LOIS DUNCAN

Duncan published *Who Killed My Daughter?* in 1992 to make sure Kait's case would not be forgotten, and although many years have gone by since the murder, Duncan tirelessly continues to seek justice for Kait.

the hospital, luckily she was soon able to bounce back to normal living. But the stroke temporarily affected typing with her left hand and gave her a lopsided smile

Duncan was determined to tell the story of her daughter's homicide to anyone who would listen. Surely there must be someone with information that could help them!

Duncan appeared on many talk shows, including *Good Morning America*, *Unsolved Mysteries*, *Inside Edition*, and *Larry King Live*. She stated the facts of the case and exposed the shortcomings of the Albuquerque police investigation. She hoped that tipsters would contact her through those TV shows. The family also created the *Kaitlyn Arquette* Web site, as another way to receive tips and share updates on the status of the case.

To this day, Kait's murder remains unsolved. Duncan still prays for a break in the case. But she has lost her faith in the American justice system.

Although Duncan still has not found all the answers she seeks about the crime, she and her husband have vowed never to stop looking for the truth. Despite her own personal agony and suffering, she pushes on. She will keep trying to solve the mystery in the hope of obtaining justice for her beloved daughter.

Chapter 9

Trailblazer and Truth Seeker

In 1992, due to death threats to the rest of the family, Duncan and Arquette moved to the Outer Banks of North Carolina. Duncan's husband retired early from Sandia National Laboratories, after working for forty years in missile design.

After what happened to Kait, Duncan could no longer find it within her to write mystery novels. She said, "Creating a fictional mystery about a young woman in jeopardy, while our own horrendous true mystery remains unsolved, is an impossible challenge."[1]

Instead, she decided to collaborate with Dr. William Roll, head of the Psychical Research Foundation, to write a nonfiction book for teenagers about parapsychology. Duncan and her co-author conducted much of their research at the

Duncan and her husband, Don Arquette, enjoy a day out on the beach.

Rhine Research Center at Duke University where Dr. Roll had many contacts.

This topic personally interested Duncan because of her daughter's murder case, and the strange coincidences between the facts of the case and the details in Duncan's novel *Don't Look Behind You*. There were chilling instances of precognition related to Kait's murder in this book. Before turning to psychic detectives to help solve Kait's murder, Duncan had believed that paranormal phenomena were fantasy. Later, however, she said, "My experiences with psychic detectives during Kait's murder investigation have forced me to change my mind about what is and isn't possible."[2]

The result of Duncan and Roll's combined efforts was *Psychic Connections* (Dell, 1995). According to a review by *Booklist* magazine, this book deals with information on ESP (extrasensory perception), out-of-body experiences, channeling and mediumship, and apparitions and hauntings, as well as psychokinesis, psychic detectives, and psychic healings.

Throughout her career, Duncan has received numerous awards. In 1992, she received the prestigious Margaret A. Edwards Award, presented by the Young Adult Library Services division of the American Library Association and the *School Library Journal* for a distinguished body of work for young adults.

A common theme in many of her books is the importance of taking responsibility for one's actions. She has used that theme in *I Know What You Did Last Summer* (Little, Brown, 1973), *Killing Mr. Griffin* (Little, Brown, 1978) and *Twisted Window* (Delacorte, 1987). Another recurrent theme in her young-adult novels is the danger of giving in to peer pressure. Teenagers today can very much relate to these themes, as they experience them on an almost daily basis.

The characters in Duncan's novels are quite believable. Duncan also has a talent for foreshadowing and has the ability to create an entertaining piece of literature. She serves up an enjoyable page-turner and manages to deliver a subtle moral message to readers without insulting their intelligence.[3]

Her books are still very popular, even though several of her best-sellers were published many years ago. Her young readers do not realize that Duncan's books were not written "yesterday."

Like many writers, Duncan realized through the years that she was competing more and more with television. She has cleverly used television's techniques of "instant gratification" to attract and hold her readers' interest. Her suspense novels grab the reader's attention—and keep them engaged from start to finish.

Although she was no longer motivated to write suspense novels, Duncan forced herself to write *Gallows Hill* (Delacorte, 1997) because she had already contracted to do so before Kait's death. This book deals with reincarnation and the Salem Witch Trials. Although it won several awards and was turned into a made-for-television movie, Duncan says she was relieved to finish it. She made a promise to herself that she would write only what she wanted to write from then on. At that time in her life, she just could not write any more mysteries.

Then, like a bolt from the blue, word came that one of Duncan's older books was going to be made into a movie! Duncan became a household name when *I Know What You Did Last Summer* hit theaters nationwide in 1997. The movie starred Freddie Prinze, Jr., and Jennifer Love Hewitt.

At first, Duncan was excited that her novel was going to the big screen. However, she changed her mind after seeing the movie. Right from the first scene, she did not recognize her novel. Setting, characters, and plot had been changed. Also, there was a heavy heaping of violent behavior and sordid scenes, which were not from the book.

Despite her distaste for the movie, it was a box office hit. Duncan made it clear in interviews that she was disgusted with the violence. She says the movie version is far more gruesome than the book she wrote and was unrecognizable to her.

Right from the first scene, she did not recognize her novel.

After all of the media attention died down, Duncan realized what she wanted to do with the rest of her life. Since the publication of

Who Killed My Daughter? she had been contacted by many people who also believed that their own loved ones' murder cases had not been investigated properly by the police. Families reached out to her in droves, sending letters and e-mails. Like Duncan, these people were desperate for answers.

Duncan had an inspired idea. In 1998, Duncan and her husband created a Web site called *Real Crimes*. They would work together to post information and bring to light the facts of unsolved homicides and missing persons cases. The Web site postings point out discrepancies in murder investigations.

Due to the attention and media pressure brought about by the *Real Crimes* Web site, some of the cases were reopened. Better still some cases have ultimately been solved. The Web site is also a valuable resource for investigative reporters and television shows.

Keeping her promise to herself to write only what made her happy, Duncan changed course a bit and wrote the text for a few picture books. She also edited three short-story anthologies for Simon & Schuster—*Night Terrors* (1996), *Trapped* (1998), and *On the Edge* (2000).

In November 2004, Duncan and her husband moved to Sarasota, Florida, the town where Duncan grew up. She has always loved the beach and the coast, and considers it her real home. Duncan says, "I'm back to the place where I started, walking the beaches of my childhood, soothed by the rhythm of the waves and cries of the gulls."[4]

Now grandparents, Duncan and her husband can be extremely proud of their life accomplishments and especially of their four surviving children. Robin, Kerry, Brett, and Donnie, are very creative artists in their own right.

Duncan recently published a book of poetry, *Seasons of the Heart* (iUniverse, 2007). Not many people know that she is a poet. All of her life Duncan has recorded many of the events from her life in verse. From the time she was a little girl, she was writing poetry. She saved all of it. *Seasons of the Heart* is a collection of poems intermingled with short passages from her life story.

> **Not many people know that Duncan is a poet.**

Duncan's life as a writer has put her in the limelight and has been deeply rewarding. As an award-winning author of more than fifty books and the creator of more than three hundred stories and articles, Duncan has contributed to the lives and minds of the young.

Duncan still takes time to give back to others. She is often a keynote speaker at conventions of school librarians and English teachers and volunteers as a counselor at the Women's Resource Center of Sarasota.

Solving Kait's murder is still her highest priority. And Duncan continues to use her gift of writing

Duncan signs a copy of 2007's *Seasons of the Heart* for a young fan.

in this passionate pursuit. She is driven to find answers to Kait's cold case, and the cases of other families who are in the same agonizing situation.

On behalf of countless others, she strives to bring killers to justice. Through the *Real Crimes* Web site, she battles alongside others to expose police cover-ups and corruption. She selflessly devotes time to families of crime victims who, like her, are searching for answers to heartbreaking questions.

Duncan, now in her seventies, also continues to write regularly. She is currently working on *The Tally Keeper*, a sequel to *Who Killed My Daughter?*, as well as two sequels to her chapter book, *Hotel for Dogs*.

Duncan's daily prayer is that one day the mystery of her daughter's death might be solved. But like the pages and storyline of a good book, she also knows that the future is unpredictable. Duncan says it best: "Life, itself, is the greatest mystery of all."[5]

In Her Own Words

The following interview with Lois Duncan was conducted by the author via e-mail in the spring of 2007.

Who is your favorite author?

There are too many to name. I read voraciously and learn from everything I read. My reaction ranges from, "I wish I'd written that!" to "I'll learn from this author's mistakes."

Do you have a set writing process?

I get up in the morning, brush my teeth, fix breakfast for my husband and me, and go to the computer. I work until it's time to fix dinner, with occasional time out to go to the grocery store, run laundry, etc.

What is your favorite part of the writing process?

Completing the final draft and writing "The End."

Where do you find your inspiration?

My plots for fiction are a combination of personal experience and imagination.

In your travels around the country speaking about writing, are there any people that stand out in your mind?

At each of those conferences, I meet wonderful teachers and librarians, and also other authors. I've become close friends with many of those people, because of our common interests. Ann Rule and Tony Hillerman wrote endorsements for *Who Killed My Daughter?* and I can never thank them enough for that. Authors Lois Lowry, Judy Blume, and Lurlene McDonald, and educator Joan Kaywell wrote blurbs for my book of poetry, *Seasons of the Heart*. I never would have known those people if I hadn't met them at conferences.

Who is your favorite character from your books?

That's impossible to answer. It's like being asked to name your favorite child.

What are the major themes of your body of work?

A basic theme that has inadvertently found its way into almost all of my young adult suspense novels is the importance of taking responsibility for one's actions.

What are your plans for the future, in terms of writing for teenagers?

I have no immediate plans to return to that genre.

What are you working on now?

The Tally Keeper, which is the sequel to *Who Killed My Daughter?*

Who are your heroes?

The families of murdered children who, instead of allowing themselves to become disabled by grief, continue to live productive lives and to investigate their children's unsolved cases long after the police have dropped out.

What is your best advice to aspiring writers?

Just sit down and do it. Writing is a self-taught craft. It comes with practice. There are no shortcuts.

If your peers were to describe you in one word, what do you think that one word would be?

Tenacious.

What has been the most surprising outcome from your life as an author?

The fact that my books have remained in print for so long. Kids today are still reading and enjoying books of mine that were published thirty-five years ago and don't seem to realize they weren't written yesterday.

Chronology

1934—Lois Duncan Steinmetz is born on April 28, in Philadelphia, Pennsylvania.

1937—Lois's brother, Bill, is born.

1939—The Steinmetz family settles in Sarasota, Florida.

1947—Lois's first story is published in *Calling All Girls* magazine.

1952—Lois graduates from Sarasota High School; enters Duke University.

1953—Drops out of college and marries Joseph "Buzz" Cardozo.

1954—Duncan's daughter, Robin, is born.

1956—Duncan's daughter, Kerry, is born.

1958—Duncan's first novel, *Debutante Hill*, is published and wins the Seventeenth Summer Literary Award.

1960—Duncan's son, Brett, is born.

1962—Duncan divorces and moves to Albuquerque, New Mexico.

1965—Duncan marries Donald Wayne Arquette, an electrical engineer, on July 15.

1966—*Ransom* is published and nominated for the Edgar Allan Poe Award.

1967—Duncan's son, Donald, Jr., is born.

1968—*They Never Came Home* is published and nominated for the Edgar Allan Poe Award.

1970—Duncan's daughter, Kaitlyn, is born.

1971—Duncan becomes faculty lecturer at the University of New Mexico; *A Gift of Magic*, Duncan's first novel about the paranormal, is published; *Hotel for Dogs* is published.

1974—*Down a Dark Hall* is published.

1976—*Summer of Fear* is published and receives the Dorothy Canfield Fisher Award.

1977—Duncan graduates with a BA in English from the University of New Mexico.

1978—*Killing Mr. Griffin* is published and named a *New York Times* "Best Book for Children."

1979—*Daughters of Eve* is published.

1981—*Stranger With My Face* is published and named a *New York Times* "Outstanding Book of the Year."

1984—*The Third Eye* is published and receives the West Australian Young Readers Award.

1985—*Locked in Time* is published and named an IRA-CBA Children's Choice.

1987—*The Twisted Window* is published and named a Parents' Choice Honor Book for Literature.

1988—Duncan and her daughter, Robin Arquette, collaborate on *Songs from Dreamland*, a book and recording of original lullabies. Duncan writes the lyrics; Robin composes the music and performs the vocals.

1989—*Don't Look Behind You* is published and receives the Parents' Choice Book Award; Duncan's daughter, Kaitlyn Arquette, is murdered in Albuquerque, New Mexico.

1992—*Who Killed My Daughter?* is published and named a School Library Journal "Best Book of the Year" and an ALA "Best Book for Young Adults"; Duncan receives the Margaret A. Edwards Award from the American Library Association; Duncan and her husband move to the Outer Banks of North Carolina.

1993—*The Circus Comes Home* is published with photo illustrations by Duncan's late father, Joseph Janney Steinmetz.

1995—Duncan collaborates with Dr. William Roll and *Psychic Connections* is published.

1997—The movie *I Know What You Did Last Summer* debuts; *Gallows Hill* is published.

1998—Duncan and her husband create the *Real Crimes* Web site, www.realcrimes.com.

2004—Duncan and her husband return to Sarasota, Florida, Duncan's childhood home.

2007—*Seasons of the Heart*, Duncan's life in poetry, is published and receives the Reader-Views Literary Award.

2009—The movie *Hotel for Dogs* is released (Dreamworks).

Selected Works by Lois Duncan

Young Adult Novels

1957   *Love Song for Joyce; Debutante Hill*

1958   *A Promise for Joyce*

1960   *The Middle Sister*

1962   *Game of Danger*

1965   *Season of the Two-Heart*

1966   *Ransom*

1968   *They Never Came Home*

1970   *Peggy*

1971   *A Gift of Magic*

1973   *I Know What You Did Last Summer*

1974   *Down a Dark Hall*

1976   *Summer of Fear*

1978   *Killing Mr. Griffin*

1979   *Daughters of Eve*

1981   *Stranger With My Face*

1984   *The Third Eye*

1985   *Locked in Time*

1987   *The Twisted Window*

1989   *Don't Look Behind You*

1997   *Gallows Hill*

Chapter Books

1971   *Hotel for Dogs*

1988   *Wonder Kid Meets the Evil Lunch Snatcher*

2009   *News for Dogs*

Picture Books

1959   *The Littlest One in the Family*

1962   *Silly Mother; Giving Away Suzanne*

1983   *The Terrible Tales of Happy Days School; From Spring to Spring*

1985   *Horses of Dreamland*

1988   *Songs from Dreamland*

1989   *The Birthday Moon*

1993   *The Circus Comes Home*

1996   *The Magic of Spider Woman*

1999   *The Longest Hair in the World*

2000   *I Walk at Night*

2002   *Song of the Circus*

Nonfiction

1969   *Major Andre: Brave Enemy*

1979   *How to Write and Sell Your Personal Experiences*

1992   *Who Killed My Daughter?*

1995   *Psychic Connections*

Autobiography

1982   Chapters: My Growth as a Writer

2007   Seasons of the Heart

Adult Novels

1966   Point of Violence

1974   When the Bough Breaks

Edited Anthologies

1996   Night Terrors

1998   Trapped!

2000   On the Edge

Chapter Notes

Chapter 1. An Important Visitor

1. Lois Duncan, *Something About the Author Autobiography Series* (Detroit, Mich.: Thomson Gale, 1986), vol. 2, p. 69.
2. Ibid.
3. Personal interview with Lois Duncan, April 5, 2007.
4. Duncan, *Something About the Author*, pp. 67–69.
5. Ibid, p. 68.
6. MacKinlay Kantor, *Andersonville* (New York: Penguin, 1964), back cover.
7. Lois Duncan, *Seasons of the Heart* (Lincoln, Nebr.: iUniverse, 2007), second page after inside front cover.
8. Personal interview with Lois Duncan, April 5, 2007.
9. Joan Griffith, "Trailblazer: Lois Duncan, Part I," *Attitudes Magazine*, March/April 2006.

Chapter 2. Little Girl Writer

1. Lois Duncan, *Something About the Author Autobiography Series* (Detroit, Mich.: Thomson Gale, 1986), vol. 2, p. 67.
2. Ibid, p. 68.
3. Lois Duncan, "My Mother" (printed here with permission from the author).

4. Duncan, *Something About the Author*, p. 68.

5. Jamie N., "Interview With Author: Lois Duncan," *Teen Ink*, 2001, <http://teenink.com/Past/2001/January/Interviews/LoisDuncan.html> (February 26, 2007).

6. Lois Duncan, "The Song of Life" (printed here with permission from the author).

Chapter 3. The Teen Years

1. Personal interview with Lois Duncan, April 5, 2007.

2. Ibid.

3. Ibid.

4. Ibid.

5. Ibid.

6. Lois Duncan, *Seasons of the Heart* (Lincoln, Nebr.: iUniverse, 2007), p. 17.

7. Cosette Kies, *Presenting Lois Duncan* (New York: Twayne, 1993), p. 4.

8. Personal interview with Lois Duncan, April 5, 2007.

9. Ibid.

10. Ibid.

Chapter 4. Duke University and Falling in Love

1. Lois Duncan, *Something About the Author Autobiography Series* (Detroit, Mich.: Thomson Gale, 1986), vol. 2, p. 70.

2. Ibid.

3. Ibid.

4. Lois Duncan, "The Faithful Wife" (printed here with permission from the author).

5. Duncan, p. 71.

Chapter 5. Single and Struggling

1. Lois Duncan, *Something About the Author Autobiography Series* (Detroit, Mich.: Thomson Gale, 1986), vol. 2, p. 72.
2. Ibid.
3. Ibid, p. 73.
4. Personal interview with Lois Duncan, April 5, 2007.

Chapter 6. Newlywed Again

1. Personal interview with Lois Duncan, April 5, 2007.
2. Ibid.

Chapter 7. Hitting the Books

1. Lois Duncan, *Something About the Author Autobiography Series* (Detroit, Mich.: Thomson Gale, 1986), vol. 2, p. 75.
2. Personal e-mail from Lois Duncan, June 22, 2008.
3. Personal interview with Lois Duncan, April 5, 2007.
4. Cosette Kies, *Presenting Lois Duncan* (New York: Twayne, 1993), p. 65.
5. Lois Duncan, *Killing Mr. Griffin* (Boston: Little, Brown, 1978), p. 5.

Chapter 8. Tragedy Strikes

1. Lois Duncan, *Who Killed My Daughter?* (New York: Delacorte, 1992), p. 20.

2. Lois Duncan, personal letter to Kimberly Campbell, October 26, 2006.

3. Cosette Kies, *Presenting Lois Duncan* (New York: Twayne, 1993), pp. 114–115.

4. Lois Duncan. *Seasons of the Heart* (Lincoln, Nebr.: iUniverse, 2007), p. 66.

5. Personal e-mail from Lois Duncan, June 22, 2008.

6. Scott Sandlin, "Mom Writes on About Daughter's Death," *Albuquerque Journal*, October 18, 2000, <http://www.realcrimes. com/Arquette/WHERE_ARE_THEY_NOW.htm> (May 22, 2007).

Chapter 9. Trailblazer and Truth Seeker

1. Joan Griffith, "Trailblazer: Lois Duncan, Part I," *Attitudes Magazine*, March/April 2006.

2. Ted Hipple, ed., *Writers for Young Adults* (New York: Charles Scribner's Sons, 1997), vol. 1, p. 398, retrieved from Gale Group, *Song for Ophelia*, Melysa Thompson, April 4, 2006, <http://eve7k.com/ophelia/author/ author_7.php> (May 15, 2007).

3. Cosette Kies, *Presenting Lois Duncan* (New York: Twayne, 1993), pp. 119–121.

4. Lois Duncan, *Seasons of the Heart* (Lincoln, Nebr.: iUniverse, 2007), p. 69.

5. Lois Duncan, "Lois Duncan: Autobiographical Update (2003)," *Song for Ophelia*, Melysa Thompson, 2006, <http://eve7k.com/ ophelia/articles/pdf_files/something_author_ revised.pdf > (April 7, 2008).

Glossary

advance—Money a publisher pays an author before a book is published.

Andersonville—A south Georgia town notorious for its Confederate prison, where more than twelve thousand soldiers died during the Civil War.

anthology—A collection of selected literary pieces, such as stories or poems.

bridge—A card game.

Civil War—The war in the United States between the Union (the North) and the Confederacy (the South) from 1861 to 1865.

civilian—A person who is not on active duty with a military, police, or firefighting organization.

cold case—A criminal investigation by a law enforcement agency that has not been solved for a long time and, as a result, has been closed from further regular investigations.

darkroom—A room with no light or with a safelight used to process photographs.

dormitory—Living quarters for students, most often found at colleges.

home economics—A class that teaches the art and science of homemaking.

Korean War—The 1950–1953 conflict between communist North Korea and The Republic of South Korea that also involved the United States and China.

mafia—A group of people who are secretly involved in illegal activities such as gambling, drug-dealing, and prostitution.

peer pressure—When others try to influence how you act or force you to do something.

precognition—Knowledge of something in advance of its occurrence.

pseudonym—A false name used in place of an author's real name.

Pueblo—A member of a group of American Indian peoples of the southwestern United States.

Pulitzer Prize—A prestigious award given in various categories (journalism, literature, music, and art) and originally established by Joseph Pulitzer.

sand dunes—Swells of sand that are produced by wind.

scholarship—Money granted to students to pay tuition costs and college expenses.

veteran—A person who formerly served in the armed forces.

World War II—A global military battle that lasted from 1939 to 1945.

Further Reading

Albert, Lisa Rondinelli. *Lois Lowry: The Giver of Stories and Memories*. Berkeley Heights, N.J.: Enslow Publishers, Inc., 2008.

Casil, Amy Sterling. *Lois Duncan*. New York: Rosen Publishing Group, 2005.

Jones, Jen. *Judy Blume: Fearless Storyteller for Teens*. Berkeley Heights, N.J.: Enslow Publishers, Inc., 2009.

Kies, Cosette N. *Presenting Lois Duncan*. Detroit, Mich.: Thomson Gale, 1994.

Internet Addresses

Lois Duncan's Official Web site
http://loisduncan.arquettes.com

Lois Duncan Red Room Web site
http://www.redroom.com/author/lois-duncan

Who Killed Kait Arquette?
http://kaitarquette.arquettes.com

Real Crimes
http://www.realcrimes.com

Robin Arquette
http://www.lullabysongs.net

Index

A

"A Graduate in the Family," 58
American Library Association, 70, 75
Andersonville, 11
Arquette, Brett, 41, 49, 79
Arquette, Donald Jr., 52, 79
Arquette, Donald W.
  marriage, 48–49
  murder investigations by, 67, 78
  retirement, 73
  as supportive husband, 56
Arquette, Kaitlyn
  birth of, 52
  murder of, 65–72, 75, 79
Arquette, Kerry, 38, 49, 79
Arquette, Lois Duncan Steinmetz
  adolescence, 23–32
  births, 15
  births of children, 38, 41, 52
  childhood/family life, 15–22

  dating, 28–29
  divorce, 42
  family life/adulthood, 37–38, 58, 61
  grandchildren, 61
  as loner, 20, 34
  marriages, 36, 49
  work ethic, 21
Arquette, Robin
  adoption of, 49
  artistic career, 61–62, 79
  birth, 38
  at Kait's funeral, 65
  royalty check, accidental disposal of, 44–45

B

Basler, Christia, 29

C

Calling All Girls magazine, 9, 21
careers
  editorial, 30, 43–44
  lectures, 54, 56
  teaching, 54, 56
  writing (*See* writing career)
car purchase, 32
censorship, 40, 50
contests, 44–45

Cordozo, Joseph "Buzz,"
36–38, 40–41, 43
creativity
downtime and, 34–35
family gift of, 15, 17,
24, 79
practical applications
of, 44–45
sorrow and, 52
crime, organized, 66

D
Darling, Sumner, 29, 31
Debutante Hill, 38–40,
59
Don't Look Behind You,
59, 62–65, 75
Duke University, 32–36,
56, 75

E
Edgar Allan Poe Award,
52
editing career, 30, 43–44
education
college, 32–36, 54–56
high school, 24, 30,
32
kindergarten, 17, 19
scholarships, 33–34

F
"Fairy in the Woods," 7
financial issues, 42–47
Foley, Perle Duncan,
24–25
From Spring to Spring, 58

G
Gallows Hill, 59, 76
gender inequality, 30, 38
Good Housekeeping, 13,
49, 58

H
health issues, 70
Home Economics Report,
26
Hotel for Dogs, 53, 81

I
*I Know What You Did
Last Summer*, 61,
76–77
inspiration, 21, 83
*I've Been Waiting For
You*, 59

K
Kantor, MacKinlay,
8–12, 20
Killing Mr. Griffin, 59,
76
Korean War, 28, 30

L
Ladies' Home Journal, 7,
49
lectures, 54, 56
"Love in March," 29
lullabies, 61–62

M
magazines
Calling All Girls, 9, 21
confession stories,
45–47, 49, 50

Good Housekeeping, 13, 49, 58
illustration of, 56
Ladies' Home Journal, 7, 49
parent's work in, 15
rejection by, 7
sale, first, 10, 22
Senior Prom, 26
Seventeen, 13, 28
stories preferred by, 8
submissions to, 7, 21, 50
managing editor, 30
Mandell, Arnold, 28
Margaret A. Edwards Award, 75
murder investigations, 65–72, 78–81
"My Mother," 19–20

N
Nguyen, Dung Ngoc, 66–69

P
parapsychology, 73–75
photography, 16, 24, 25, 45, 56
"P.S. We Are Fine," 9
Psychic Connections, 75
psychic detectives, 67, 75

R
Ransom, 50
Real Crimes Web site, 78, 81
"Return," 28

Ringling Brothers Barnum and Bailey Circus, 24
Roll, William, 73, 75
royalties, 28, 40, 43, 45

S
Sandia National Laboratories, 48, 73
Sarasota High School, 24, 32
school newspaper editor, 30
Season of the Two-Heart, 43
Seasons of the Heart, 12, 28, 79
Senior Prom magazine, 26
Seventeen magazine, 13, 28
Seventeen Summer Literary Award, 28
"Seventeenth Summer Literary Contest," 38
social expectations, women/1950's, 35
social inequality, 30, 38
Songs From Dreamland, 61–62, 65
Steinmetz, Joseph Janney, 15, 16, 24, 25, 33
Steinmetz, Lois Duncan Foley, 15, 26, 33, 52
Steinmetz, William birth, 16
childhood/family life, 16–17, 24

as emotional support, 43, 47, 78
Stranger in Our House, 59
Summer of Fear, 59
supernatural stories, 7, 58, 68, 73–75

T

talk shows, 72
teaching career, 54, 56
television, 58–59, 76–78
The Circus Comes Home, 25–26
"The Faithful Wife," 37
"The First Snow," 69–70
"The Song of Life," 21
The Tally Keeper, 81
"The Year I Won the Contest," 49
They Never Came Home, 52
True Story contest, 44
Twisted Window, 76

U

U. S. Air Force, 36, 48
University of New Mexico, 54, 56, 63

W

Who Killed My Daughter?, 70–72, 78, 81
World War II, 16
writer's block, 52–53, 69
writing career. *See also* specific titles.

awards, 28, 40, 52, 70, 75
compensation, 10, 22, 28, 40, 43, 45
confession stories, 45–47, 49, 50
critiques, 9
first published story, 22
magazines (*See* magazines)
pen name, 23
poetry, 12, 28, 79
popularity, 52, 76
post-divorce, 42–44
rejections, 7–8, 26
supernatural stories, 7, 58, 68, 73–75
teen novels, 50, 58–59
titles list, 89–91
writing process, 82
writing style
characters, 76
downtime, creativity and, 34–35
overview, 7–11
realism, 11
skills, mastery of, 50, 58
themes, 38, 44, 76, 83